The Ant's Journey

Story by Janie Spaht Gill, Ph.D.
Illustrations by Bob Reese

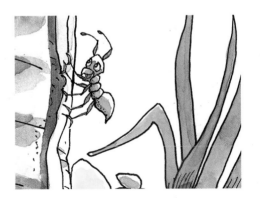

DOMINIE PRESS

Pearson Learning Group

he ant left the anthill
take a look around.

ook!" he said.
t's a tall, gray tree.
at's the first thing I found."

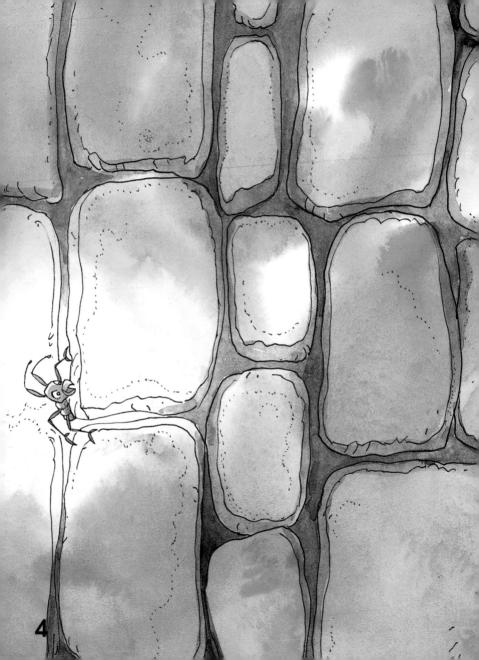

4

The ant left the tree
to take a look around.

"Look!" he said.
"It's a big, red chimney.
That's the second thing
I found."

The ant left the chimney
to take a look around.

"Look!" he said.
"It's a big, blue ocean.
That's the third thing
I found."

7

The ant left the ocean
to take a look around.

"Look!" he said.
"It's a big, orange bridge.
That's the fourth thing
I found."

The ant left the bridge
to take a look around.

"Look!" he said.
"It's a big, white snow bank.
That's the fifth thing I found."

10

The ant left the snow bank
to take a look around.

"Look!" he said.
"It's a big, yellow moon.
That's the sixth thing
I found."

The ant left the moon
to take a look around.

"Look!" he said.
"It's a big, brown log.
That's the seventh thing
I found."

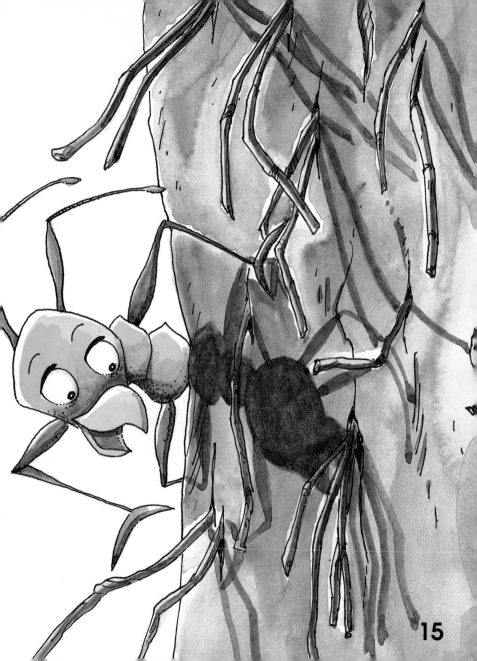

The ant left the log
to take a look around.

"Look!" he said.
"It's a big, green mounta
That's the eighth thing
I found."

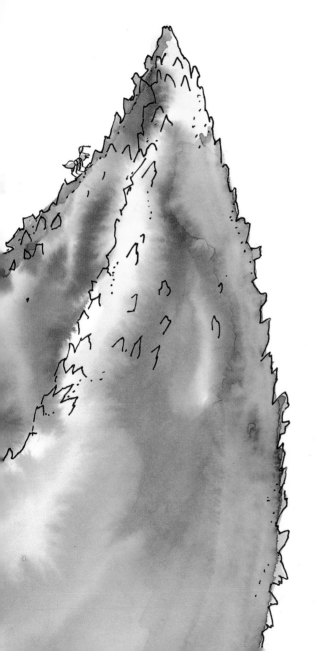

When the ant reached
the end, he took
a look around, and this is
what he saw, from the top
as he looked down.

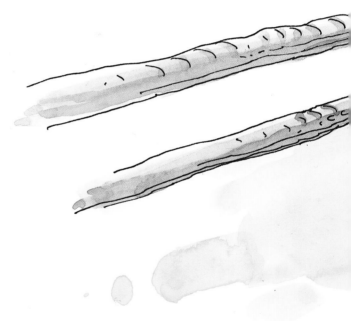

19

Now find the tree, the chimney
the ocean, the bridge,
the snow bank, the moon,
the log, and the mountain.

21

Curriculum Extension Activities

- Use this opportunity to have the children talk about what life would be like if they were ants. Write their suggestions on the board. Then have them fold a sheet of paper into fourths, cutting the paper on the folded line to make a three-page book. The first page will include the title and a child's name listed as the author and illustrator. On each of the other pages, the children will write and illustrate something they would do if they were an ant. For example, "I'd live in the ground."

- Have the children draw a scarecrow on a sheet of paper. Then have them color the scarecrow and label the tree, the chimney, the ocean, the bridge, the snow bank, the moon, the log, and the mountain.

- Use this opportunity to teach "first, second," etc. by inviting the children to look at the pictures in the book and retell the story, adding the appropriate word at the beginning of each sentence: "First, the ant climbed the gray tree," etc.

About the Author

Dr. Janie Spaht Gill brings twenty-five years of teaching experience to her books for young children. During her career thus far, she has taught at every grade level, from kindergarten through college. Gill has a Ph.D. in reading education, with a minor in creative writing. She is currently residing in Lafayette, Louisiana with her husband, Richard. Her fresh, humorous topics are inspired by the things her students say in the classroom. Gill was voted the 1999-2000 Louisiana Elementary Teacher of the Year for her outstanding work in primary education.

Copyright © 2003 by Pearson Education, Inc., publishing as Dominie Press, an imprint of Pearson Learning Group, 299 Jefferson Road, Parsippany, NJ 07054.

All rights reserved. No part of this book may be reproduced or transmitted in any form or by any means, electronic, or mechanical, including photocopying, recording, or by any information storage and retrieval system, without permission in writing from the publisher. For information regarding permission(s), write to Rights and Permissions Department.

Softcover Edition ISBN 0-7685-2155-6
Library Bound Edition ISBN 0-7685-2463-6

Printed in Singapore
4 5 6 7 8 9 10   10 09 08 07

Dominie
Press

Pearson Learning Group

1-800-321-3106
www.pearsonlearning.com